CONTRACTOR BY SURPRISE

CONTRACTOR BY SURPRISE

TERRI WALKER PULLEN

Copyright © 2021 by Terri Walker Pullen

ISBN   Softcover   978-1-953537-64-5

Bible translation used: *King James Version*

All rights reserved. No part of this book may be reproduced or transmitted in any form or by any means, electronic or mechanical, including photocopying, recording, or by any information storage and retrieval system without express written permission from the author, except in the case of brief quotations embodied in critical reviews and certain other non-commercial uses permitted by copyright law.

Printed in the United States of America.

To order additional copies of this book, contact:
Bookwhip
1-855-339-3589
www.bookwhip.com

CONTENTS

Dedication vii

Acknowledgments ix

Foreword xi

Introduction xiii

Chapter 1   What Do You Mean I'm Laid Off? 1

Chapter 2   A Plan B! 3

Chapter 3   Plan B Formation 7

Chapter 4   Promising Days Ahead 15

Chapter 5   A Totally Different Education 17

Chapter 6   American Institute of Architects (AIA) Tips 23

Chapter 7   A Mission Accomplished 27

Chapter 8   Encouragement for New Beginnings 29

DEDICATION

I dedicate this book to my beloved husband, Richard H. Pullen, Jr., who has always proven to be an outstanding demonstration of true integrity and man of superior work ethics who continually reflects passion and dedication in providing quality construction building services. Not only have I found you to be a great construction builder, but more importantly, a great man of God who faithfully serves in the marketplace ministry. I love you forever and will always try to support the work that God has assigned to your hands.

—Your wife, Terri

ACKNOWLEDGMENTS

First and foremost, I acknowledge Almighty God and my Lord and Saviour, Jesus Christ, who so graciously granted me the faith, wisdom, and knowledge to write this book. I also acknowledge my husband of more than twenty-five years, who has exemplified the meaning of James 2:14 KJV, in that "faith without works is dead," and has steadfastly worked his faith into building this construction company. I further acknowledge Dr. Patrick L. Wooden, Sr., Pastor, Upper Room Church of God in Christ, Raleigh, NC, who continuously built my faith by preaching the true gospel of Jesus Christ. I also acknowledge my mother, Deloris Alexander Walker, who always reminded me at various times throughout the years to jot down notes to include in my book. Last but not least, I acknowledge Mr. George York, Jr. for being kind enough to take time from his busy schedule to write the foreword of this book. Thank you all so much for the vital roles you have played in helping me to produce this work of authorship. May God always bless you richly for many, many years to come.

FOREWORD

As I sit here today, we as a nation are about to begin our sixth year of recession-like economy (I say recession-like, because everyone feels as if we are still in a recession, regardless of the fact that the economists would tell us the recession ended in June 2009). As a resident of Raleigh, NC, I am told we have it "better than most" as our regional unemployment has dipped to near 8 percent better than the national average, and our home prices haven't crashed *as bad* as they have elsewhere in the country, and we will be the "last in and first out" of this national economic crisis we have all battled with over the past six years. We are at or near the top of almost every list of city/regional rankings as the best place to live, work, play, and raise a family. However, this provides little consolation for those of us here because we know that despite our good fortune, we are still struggling just as the rest of our fellow Americans are. With nearly 40,000 people out of work in the Research Triangle Region, and more qualified workers graduating and staying in the area from our wonderful local colleges and universities, it is hard to see how this will improve greatly over the next couple of years ahead. Hundreds of qualified people apply for almost any advertised position in our area whether or not they are currently living here. We are beginning to see signs of improvement, but the pace at which things are improving today will not excite too many people who are out of work. So if you are reading this now, and you are one of the unlucky ones fighting each day for your next opportunity, read on, as this is a story of determination, redemption, and faith that may provide you with some newfound hope.

My opportunity to write this foreword came about because of my relationship with the Raleigh Business and Technology Center and the fine people running that program, including Mr. Bob Robinson. The Raleigh Business and Technology Center recruited me to get involved with their program, and although I feel like I have done very little, it appears that what I have been able to do has made a positive impact on some of the participants and graduates of their various programs, but most significantly their Pacesetters program, from which Mrs. Pullen is a graduate. Mrs. Pullen challenged herself by attending this first-class business education program during her time of crisis, and she put the tools she was given to work with outstanding results, even through the recession-like period we are currently in. As you read her story, think about what you are doing to improve yourself on a daily basis to make yourself a better candidate for employment, or to make your business a better candidate for long-term survival. Mrs. Pullen can serve as a beacon of hope for those of you who have thrown up your hands to the sky to ask, "What now?" as she is an example of resiliency and hope that with the proper attention to your goals you can impact your future and the course you are on.

—George S. York, Jr. York Properties, Inc.
McDonald York Building Company
Raleigh, NC

INTRODUCTION

Unfortunately, losing a job is an all-too-common occurrence for many people. In *Contractor by Surprise*, I have told the story of my journey from job loss to entrepreneurship. In an endeavor to help others through my experience, I have included action steps in most chapters describing the helpful lessons I learned.

CHAPTER 1

What Do You Mean I'm Laid Off?

Have you ever thought you had your life planned just right when all of a sudden it was as though someone snatched the floor from underneath your feet? Suddenly, your world seemed to be falling apart at bullet speed?

This happened to me when I lost my job and found myself wondering, *What in the world just happened?* My supervisor called me into her office.

"Terri, I'm afraid I have some bad news," she said, "You are being terminated. Today is your last day of work."

I was completely shocked! I thought that I had everything strategically planned. My career plan was to stay on course with completing my Information Technology degree and advance in the workplace into a Computer Network Administration position, potentially an engineer. I had already completed several required college classes in computer hardware, network administration, typology, and computer programming at my local community college.

Additionally, I had also completed several certifications in the Information/Networking Technology college curriculums and only had a few more classes remaining before completing the degree program that I had so earnestly aspired to achieve. While in the process of earning this education, I was fortunate to have been hired at one of the world's most famous and prestigious information technology companies. This was a worldwide organization well known in the technology industry.

Working at this particular firm, I would imagine, was like being employed at the nation's White House because of all the upscale perks that came with full-time employment at this particular company. All employees had their own private offices. There were several on-campus lunch facilities, a school for working families with small children, and even a gymnasium with swimming pools and healthcare clinics.

Nonetheless, after having worked for this company for a number of years, I found myself being terminated! I had always considered myself to be a standout among employees in the department. In doing so, my objective was to become the next department manager. I habitually came to work early, stayed late, and worked on weekends for several projects. I received employee pay raises annually because of my excellent evaluations and reviews. During the month of December, what I consider the most special time of the year, there I was being laid off. Some Christmas present, I thought. Like many other children, my kids were also expecting to have Christmas presents to open on Christmas morning, but now, suddenly, I was without income or health benefits.

Action Steps: The first thing you must do after being laid off is stop spending unnecessary money. Only spend money required for living expenses. The best preparation beforehand in the event that you lose your job is to have a right relationship with the Lord Jesus Christ so that he can give you a workable plan of action.

CHAPTER 2

A Plan B!

I'll never forget the day when I came home early from the office with the very uneasy feeling of not knowing what to do next. It was clear to me that I was so busy planning my career goals that I forgot to have a plan B. Well, it was time to think about becoming creative really fast for plan B. I came home from work earlier than usual on the afternoon that I was laid off, and my mother, who was visiting at the time, looked up at me with surprise and asked what I was doing home so early. When I told her that I had gotten terminated, she said, "What?!"

Shortly afterward, my husband came home to pick up a few construction tools from our residential storage area in the back yard. When he came into the house, I told him what had happened, and he just acted as if I had not said a word. It was business as usual for him. He acted as if everything was all right. I was amazed at his response to remain stable and nonchalant about the bad news of my job layoff. Despite the layoff, my family and I still had a lovely Christmas, regardless of all the uncertainties that faced us in the coming months.

I must admit the unknown felt overwhelmingly frightening at times. Since my income had been significantly reduced, continued tuition was impossible. Needless to say, outstanding degree classes had to be cancelled. There I was in the prime of life, having to start over again.

The one comfort for me was the fact that I had served God with all my heart. In having done so, I recalled one of his promises to provide all my needs according to Philippians 4:19, KJV. My husband and I had always tried to make it a high priority to pay tithes and offerings to our local church in supporting the work of the Lord. Having this track record was the one thing that brought me peace in my current dilemma. This brought me confidence, because in Philippians 4:19, the Lord promised to supply our needs once we have committed to supporting his work through monetary giving at the local church levels. Therefore, this provided confidence in knowing that I had been a giver to support God's work through paying tithes and offerings regularly, and I knew that with such a track record, God would also supply my needs as well. Another confidence for me was the fact that my husband never showed any negative emotions about what seemed to be a very detrimental experience. He always acted as if nothing had changed—this was also a huge relief.

At the time, I didn't know why he was so calm, but later he told me that he had been praying, asking God for my help in his business. He said, "Terri, you know, we are going to see what this business does. I had been praying to God for your help in the business, because I cannot do the construction estimating, building, and handle the paper work and manage the money all at the same time. This is the reason I believe that the business has struggled and has not made money. What I need is someone with intelligence to operate and manage the business. So you just get ready to handle a lot of stuff!" I was speechless and could not say a word. All I could do at this point in time was trust and obey.

Prior to this I had showed no interest, since the cash flow previously generated from the business was often too minimal, causing ongoing panic for me. Therefore, I genuinely had no interest in being employed in what always appeared to be a struggling construction business. My husband, Richard, had always been highly skilled in carpentry and construction building, but for many years, the income from this trade was meager and insufficient for supporting and raising a family. We had a moderate size house with a mortgage and utility bills, as well as three growing kids, Tosha, Derrick, and Rachel, who all regularly needed clothes, school supplies, and extracurricular activity equipment or uniforms for various school activities, in which they were each involved.

Tosha played basketball and volleyball throughout her school years through high school and was awarded scholarships into college. Derrick played football from little league through high school as well, and his athletic talent also awarded him scholarship entrance into college. Rachel had no athletic aspirations, but instead had a love for musical instruments and band. She always worked hard in school and entered college at the top of her class. We had three beautiful, bright kids; a great family, but we were in need of all the normal things a regular family must have to successfully raise and educate young children.

Therefore, the thought of working full-time in my husband's struggling construction business was absolutely foolish logic for me. I had always been the one with the stable income, health insurance, and benefits, which was all the more reason why I had no desire to work in a young, small construction business, because my previous experience in attempting to work in the family business had only proved to be a life of financial hardships (We had lost cars and homes, so it was like torture for me to be forced back into employment through our small family business).

Action Steps: Don't be afraid to consider and pursue alternate ideas. Take an inventory of which things are absolutely necessary for you and your family, and which things are not. Then move forward with a new plan of action to pursue those alternate ideas by which you have been inspired.

CHAPTER 3

Plan B Formation

After informing my husband that I had been terminated, he gave me his interpretation of the situation then simply replied, "We are going to see what this business will do! You just get ready to handle a lot of stuff!" I had no clue as to what he was talking about in terms of handling a lot of stuff. My immediate thoughts were: *What stuff?* and,

Are you nuts? The small mom-and-pop shop construction business had never been overly busy in the first place.

Most of the time, the business struggled just to survive, and most of my husband's clients were not wealthy people at all! To make matters worse, although my husband had many good years of building experience, he did not have an important credential called a general contractor's license. This fact greatly limited his financial income, and I was still like, "Are you kidding me?!?!" and "Why is this happening to me?!?!"

Basically, all I wanted was to have a steady income again. Having nothing to lose and anticipating some type of miracle, I arranged my home office and made myself ready to answer incoming calls and type more contract proposals. The only problem was that the phone never rang, and when it did ring, it was only bill collectors harassing me for next invoice payments.

It wasn't long before several months passed—about four months, to be exact—and I still could not figure out why my husband had told me to get ready to handle a lot of stuff. After four months, the only thing I could hear was crickets! Absolutely nothing appeared to be happening after well over a quarter of the New Year, and this was turning me into a bag of nerves.

The phone had been so silent all this time that one day I decided to flip through the yellow pages and begin making cold market calls in an attempt to get new construction work orders. Despite my best efforts, more of nothing happened! By this time I started to feel very nervous and so continued seeking employment while hoping to receive new construction service calls. I strategically scheduled half the day to search the Internet, e-mail resumes, mail hardcopy resumes, and visit employment security offices, along with anything else I could do to feel as though I was putting forth earnest effort to regain steady income. The second half of the day was used to focus on construction business opportunities.

Action Steps: Be sure to strategically schedule your day for the best chances of success. You can do this by spending half the day pursuing alternative ideas and the other half seeking more steady traditional income, if necessary. Whatever you do, do not waste precious time feeling sorry for yourself! Time is always of the essence, and you cannot store it or get it back again. Once time is gone, it's gone, so make best uses of it wisely.

One day after I had checked the mailbox there was an invitation to attend a business program that was being sponsored by the city in which we resided. It did not offer a lot of information, just an invitation to forward your interest to improve your small business, and so I did. Therefore, as noted in the instructions, I forwarded a cover letter with a copy of our small business profile, which basically describes the type of services or products a business offers. Then there was the dreadful reality of the interviewing process to determine if you, as a business owner, even qualified to be a part of this special training. I'll never forget how intimidating it felt at the interview with a certain gentleman who was the interviewer. This man was an older, tall African American man in his early to mid 50's. He was fair skinned, very educated with light greenish eyes and he spoke with a deep, slow tone of voice that naturally made a person swallow hard, if he or she was trying to make an impression. In my mind, Richard and I really had not accomplished much in our small business, and to be honest, I didn't think that our small business would pass the mustard with this guy. It didn't matter what I thought because I was about to be taken into a room to be interviewed, and soon would find out if whether our business would pass the test.

After being taken into the interviewing conference room, I knew it was about to be on. I knew I had to try hard to sell my small business to this man with decision-making power; he would either let me into the program or reject me by not allowing entry on my company's behalf. So there I was left with the burden of selling Pullen and what it had to offer to the community and general buying public at large.

So the interviewing questions began. The interviewer looked at me from across the long conference table and asked, "So Mrs. Pullen, what is your business? Tell me what it is that you do." Then there were those enormous few seconds of silence that happen when you are in a competitive situation and asked this type of question, and at the same time you are trying to organize your thoughts to give an impressive, informative response. After gathering enough nerve in the heat of the moment, I began to tell the interviewer about what I believed Pullen Construction Company was; that it was a construction contracting service specializing in residential building, renovations, major repairs and restorations. I went on telling the interviewer that my husband and I had been in business for several years where we had developed a small customer base of at least thirty-five regular residential customers. We had lived in a rural area and the small community where we lived heavily depended on our services to fix people's construction problems and improve their homes and churches; and so forth and so on.

The interviewer listened attentively and the room got quiet again. When it did, I realized that I had said everything that needed to be said and could not think of anything else to fill the silence, so I just sat there looking and waiting for this interviewer's response. After several minutes, he asked, "Mrs. Pullen, what is your five-year plan for your business, do you have a business plan?" Struggling to sound confident, I replied, "Yes Sir, my five-year plan for my business is that it will be an organization operating with credentials such as a state licensure for general contractors and advanced business certifications and degrees earned from local colleges and universities. I will also hire necessary man power to efficiently manage its daily operations for better competing in the marketplace through estimating for bid opportunities with local and state government agencies, as well as, larger construction firms. As for a business plan, I am currently in the process of completing my business plan and the only outstanding pieces remaining to be completed at this time are numerical referencing data that would illustrate current and future market trends, analysis, and so forth."

The interviewer then got up from his chair and walked over to the white board and began drawing diagrams that illustrated cash flow data samples. He began to explain the importance of business components as working capital management and how it will always determine how much money a company can spend for any purpose, i.e., business operations, equipment rentals, new hire of employees and subcontractors, vacations, etc. His lesson to me was if your working capital account does not adequately reflect the means to pay for the justification of expenditures then you simply do not make the purchase! The interviewer made this point so adamant that I still remember it to this day.

One thing was clear about the interviewer, and that was he meant business, and I thought that if I could just pass his program entry interview, I would be well on my way. So we finally wrapped up the interview. I shook the interviewer's hand while thanking him for his time, and made my way out of the room. The interviewer never said a word as to whether my small business had been accepted into the Pacesetter Program, and at the time, I was simply too afraid to ask. Therefore, I decided to wait it out for a day or so before following up with a phone call. However, when I did make the phone call to learn of my small business status for this program, I was pleasantly surprised to learn that Pullen Construction Company had been approved and accepted into the 2004 Pacesetters Virtual Business Incubator Program for the city of Raleigh, North Carolina! This was a very good feeling indeed and something great to celebrate!

Not long afterward, I found myself attending a series of business classes taught by various business professionals. In this business training, every aspect of business was taught in this particular program such as marketing, accounting, human resources, business planning, and so on. Reputable city officials were found to be stakeholders of this economical development program for small business education. The city mayor, manager, and councilman were all sponsors of this event. Once participants successfully completed the nine-month series of small business modules, the Pacesetter Program ended with a televised graduation ceremony. The graduation aired on local TV channels continuously for about a year.

This graduation ceremony was a pivotal event because it was the formal presentation of new businesses to city officials, as well as to the residents living in the city who viewed the TV broadcast. It recognized business owners as being passionate enough about their particular businesses to pursue and successfully complete nine months of business education to perfect their small businesses. Additionally, after having gone through the Pacesetter Program, our business was now positioned to be recognized by other governmental agencies to which we could also offer services and products. Therefore, our small business customer base immediately increased significantly.

During these exciting times of new found hope for our small business, I was extremely fortunate to meet and establish a great business relationship with the executive director of the Raleigh Business & Technology Center. Almost immediately, the executive director began to challenge me in ways that I had never been challenged before. Once while on the elevator together, the city was in its initial planning stages of building a new convention center. On this particular day while in the elevator, the executive director suddenly asked, "Terri, what are your ideas for the new convention center?" I was like a deer caught in lights. First off, we had never built any commercial construction structures, only small residential projects. Secondly, if my memory serves me correctly, the new proposed convention center was budgeted somewhere around $90,000,000. My mind was completely blown that an executive director of business would have interest in my response on such a question. I knew that this particular business executive was a very well connected business man—a quality mentor and coach of business indeed. He knew everyone who was someone in the city, as well as, the state of North Carolina. Due to only having had residential construction building experience at the time the question was presented, I didn't have a clue about commercial design ideas for the city's new convention center. Being a complete gentleman he realized that I was too inexperienced in commercial construction building to answer the question, and kindly relieved me by saying, "Terri, you think about that and let me know." Well, the next thing I knew, my husband and I were sitting in the office of a major contracting company discussing mentorship protégé possibilities on such a project.

From there, Richard and I found ourselves in front of many business audiences, networking with vice presidents of very large construction companies, agencies, and other organizations. We were also being invited to speak to different business audiences. Our company and names were also being published in several local city newspapers, magazines, and college campus magazines.

All these things that were happening felt exciting! Approximately fifteen months after having been laid off from the workforce, my husband and I ended up being awarded one of the largest commercial construction contracts (totaling well over a million dollars), ever in the history of our construction business! We were awarded these contracts solely based on our competitive estimating efforts! Due to this wonderful program that our city sponsors for small businesses, our small business went from a mere mom-and-pop shop, operating out of our home, to hiring a labor force of more than thirty full-time employees. This was incredible and something that I had never seen coming.

Richard and I both felt shocked and nervous, but in a good way. We also felt the need to celebrate a great victory for the progress that our small construction business had made. We celebrated in our own quiet way, because we did not want to appear as being boastful, especially being new to the commercial construction industry. We did not know what it really meant and were in for the learning experience of our life! Nonetheless, we both knew and pleasantly understood that our business would never be the same again, and from that moment, people would know the name Pullen, Pullen Construction or Richard H. Pullen; and that was a very good feeling.

Action Steps: Seek out local opportunities. Promote yourself any way you can. Take advantage of all free advertising opportunities when they come your way through news reporter interviews, magazine editors, and the like. This is a wonderful way to market your business on a low budget. Also, be sure to take care of your body by staying physically fit to look the part and by eating healthy diets, exercising regularly, keeping groomed and wardrobes up to date. Small business owners cannot afford to appear sloppy to the general public. Therefore, you must remember that you are always selling your business whether stepping out on the town or going to the convenient store. Taking time to package yourself appropriately will always pay off in presenting a positive self image as a business owner or making for good conversation with potential new customers.

CHAPTER 4

Promising Days Ahead

Now we had real employees, including OSHA-certified forklift operators who had been trained and certified through our organization, along with carpenters, administrators, foremen, and general laborers. We now worked from a beautiful office space located in the metropolitan area of our city across from a major historically black college. Our office was not just any ol' office, but it was fully equipped with all the amenities of a reputable small business office.

The affordable office rent also came with computer network LANs, a break room and kitchen with vending machinery, construction plan room, conference rooms, computer lab with printers, and an executive board room. Tenants had access to all of the amenities when renting from this particular office building. I could see that my husband's intuition had finally begun to materialize. It was quite obvious that my life had changed very drastically. Now our office phone line, as well as fax lines, rang almost on an ongoing basis with *real* construction bid opportunities. Customer e-mails were coming across the Internet into our business e-mail servers twenty-four hours, seven days a week, inviting our firm to bid new contract opportunities. Moreover, we were traveling to different cities of the state conducting business presentations in competition for new contract awards.

Once, after presenting to the board of directors at one of the state's local universities, we were awarded a portion of the university's new school addition project. Our company worked under the leadership of the construction manager general contracting firm as its Project Engineer. This project was unique in that one of our company team members was assigned to the project for the duration as a type of on-the-job training opportunity.

It was a requirement for one of our staff members to live in another city close by this particular university, as a representative of our company. Our firm paid this staff member's salary, housing, utilities, and food. In turn, our employee was to learn hands-on projects, and engineering business practices in a real-world commercial building environment. This was the ideal situation for our company to learn project engineering/management in a large scale construction environment.

These new experiences made me feel as though our organization was really taking off to grow into a solid construction company. This particular project opportunity was also unique in that during the new construction of this school's new addition, my husband and I would attend monthly progress meetings, interact with project owners and state government representatives, general contracting officers who were initially awarded the overall project along with architects, engineers, and other subcontracting trade officers. This project had approximately twenty-three subcontractor tradesmen working on schedule, and the overall project value was approximately $22,000,000.

Action Steps: Think outside the box (take full advantage of mentor/protégé opportunities from more established companies to help train employees for employment roles.) This effort will help to build your company to make for a better competitor in the particular industry that your company represents. Also, take time to learn something every day.

CHAPTER 5

A Totally Different Education

As a result of our large scale contract awards, I immediately learned there would be continuous massive administration requirements. Many times, the administration was overwhelming, because the paperwork was such a new adventure and presented on a much more elevated scale. There were contractor pre-qualifications to be completed for competing on governmental contract opportunities. Once contract awards were established there were monthly progress payments that had to be accurately estimated, calculated, and submitted to either the architect—if our company was the single prime contractor—or to the prime contracting firm—if our company was the subcontracting company.

In either case, attention to detail was critical, and many ongoing deadlines needed to be met with precision, and important appointments had to be kept. I was suddenly wearing so many hats that it was difficult to keep up, but somehow I did and performed all required tasks well.

The beautiful wonder of it all was that Richard still was not yet a licensed general contractor when we won two of the biggest construction contracts in his career. We were considered the subcontractor, which is actually unlimited in terms of the amount of money a small business could earn. This was commercial construction, and so there was lots of work to do all the time just to sustain business operations. Although it was the most demanding work we had ever done, the new world of commercial construction was also the most rewarding and exciting. It was life-changing to see the kind of monthly income our company was earning. Although, tons of overhead were attached to this enlarged cash flow, at the end of the day, it still was a much more lucrative cash flow than what we had ever experienced in times past.

Now all of a sudden, I was earning on a monthly basis more than the equivalent of several of the ladies' annual salaries who worked in the same department where I had previously been employed! Life is strange in that one moment, you can feel as though you're as low as the dirt because of some misfortune you think you have had, when in reality, it's just God's way of closing one door to open a greater one.

My husband and I had absolutely no idea this type of change awaited us in our construction career. We were ecstatic about the success our business was now experiencing, and laughing all the way to the bank every thirty days. Bank tellers would stare at us because of the large checks we were depositing into our business accounts. At every deposit visit, bank tellers would look up at either Richard or me and say, "We are going to have to put a hold on this deposit."

When this first happened, I would ask, "For how long will the hold last before funds are available?" Then here came the dropping of the bomb, because the teller would say, "Funds will become available on June 7th," or something like this, only to find that the June 7th date only allowed for a portion of the whole deposit to be released. We would always have to wait several more days for the remainder of the deposited funds to become available.

Because we were under-capitalized, this was always a time of anxiety in some ways, depending upon what billings were due at the time. Once when this happened, it was right at the time of one of our payrolls to approximately thirty-three full-time employees. We had to delay distributing paychecks by one day because funds simply had not become available. Richard formed a meeting on a Friday afternoon, the scheduled day for paying employees.

He told the crews, "Guys, we do not have your paychecks today, but will be glad to meet everyone at the office building on tomorrow morning to distribute checks. We know that tomorrow is Saturday, but you will be able to cash your checks either at local banks up until noon or at the check cashing stores located throughout the city."

Thank God when our staff members were informed, everyone was very cooperative. There may have been one or two employees who murmured, but for the most part, everyone was fine with the delay, which only happened that one time out of the 24 months of the duration of those certain projects that we were working at the time.

We prospered like we had never been able to before. There was still so much to learn in this new phase of our construction business, commercial construction in particular. Having never performed construction on large scales such as multi-million dollar procurement, we had to learn all sorts of new business practices especially in the commercial construction industry.

Action Steps: Always remember to treat your employees with genuine, loving kindness, care, and respect. People are not nearly concerned about how much you know as they are about how much you care. Once employees understand that you are concerned about their wellbeing, they usually go the extra mile to work harder in being productive to show their appreciation. Therefore, it is always a good and wise investment to make your workers feel valued. Additionally, always remember to treat your business counter parts with the same genuine care and respect. Build good business relationships, even during times where the relationship, is challenged. If you continue to work in building positive business relationships it will pay off in the long run.

There were also many business certifications to acquire and maintain so that we could more effectively compete in the marketplace. Certifications included Historically Utilized Business (HUB), Minority and Woman Owned Business Enterprise (MWBE), Disadvantaged Business Enterprise (DBE), and others. We attended various contractor pre-bid meetings on an ongoing basis so that we could stay abreast of new and upcoming construction projects. Public bid proposals had to be completed, notarized, submitted, and delivered by the designated project bid deadlines. State laws had to be learned and adhered to, along with effective project management, AIA documentation, and so forth.

Further, I found myself attending executive management programs at the University of North Carolina at Chapel Hill at the Kenan-Flagler Business School and construction academies at North Carolina Central University. Again, new education we had to learn in commercial construction appeared endless, but was invaluable.

The added value in all of this was the fact that new education and business relationships were constantly being developed with other contractors and business owners. One extremely hard and expensive lesson we had to learn, however, was the fact that at one time we relied too heavily on computer technology for submitting bids. Once when we were the apparent low bidder on a state government contract, it turned out that after several weeks past, a terrible discovery was made. The discovery was that our Excel spreadsheet had an error in the total estimated sum portion of our base bid price. The application did not automatically correct the comma mistakenly placed where a decimal should have been. The end result was that all expense line items were not properly added in the total estimated sum calculation as had been presumed causing our bid to be too low to successfully perform the required work. What a disaster when this error was found!

Our company spent several months, even a few years trying to convince the project owners that it was an honest mistake when our software failed to accurately add up each individual expense line item!

The priceless lesson learned from that nightmare was to never totally rely on computers for construction bid math calculations. *Always, always* take the extra time and effort to verify total bid estimates by the old-fashion method of manually calculating mathematically. As hard as it was, fortunately, we finally were able to move pass this embarrassing contract situation. Nonetheless, the educational cost to our company in this instance was astronomically enormous in loss of projected contract service revenues, and we now understand to never allow this type of discrepancy to ever happen again. As the ole saying goes, experience is truly the best teacher!

As we moved forward with developing our small construction business, Richard set a goal and finally acquired his state builder general contracting license. Apparently, this was a major milestone for our small business.

General contracting licensure, of course, would offer more opportunities and options for our firm to perform at the commercial and residential construction levels.

It also offered the fact that we could earn proper credentials as it was important to us that our company not just be one that built structures or performed construction services, but also be a company that would embrace and appreciate formal education for the sake of delivering business excellence. In fact, after Richard acquired his general contractor's license, I pursued and completed my bachelor's of business administration degree with a minor in contract acquisitions.

Action Steps: Never totally rely on information technology, especially when calculating important estimations and computations. Make a habit to appreciate the old-fashioned way of doing math. <u>Always</u>, allow time to do a thorough job when calculating construction estimations. This will ensure better accuracy and eliminate dreadful errors. Proper time management, scheduling and organization is also key. Always set goals to include formal education as it pertains to your particular business.

CHAPTER 6

American Institute of Architects (AIA) Tips

If you are considering being an independent construction contractor, I would like to share a bit of information that will be a tremendous help, especially for minority contractors. These tips have to do with the AIA Application and Certificate for Payment Form G702 math computation, as it relates to a quick and easy way to calculate your monthly billings. In the construction contracting community, the short version of this form is actually referred to as the 'Pay App'.

More than likely, these forms will be in the electronic form and sent to you via email from the larger general contracting companies for which your company is working. When completing the AIA G702 pay application form, be sure to understand basic spreadsheet concepts such as those in Microsoft Excel. These forms work much like the mathematical computations found in the excel spreadsheets. When calculating the notorious electronic AIA G702, a trick I always use is that on the Continuation Form AIA G703 page when entering billings for the current month's period, the following practices usually allow for increased user efficiency:

- Use the *Work Completed* column to see data needing to be entered into the *Previous Application* and *This Period* columns.
- As you manually enter each dollar amount from the *This Period* column into the *Previous Application* column, always clear each line item, one line at a time, in the *This Period* column.
- Once all *Previous Application* entries have been updated, enter your current month's billings into the *This Period* column by manually typing in each new month's billing dollar amount.
- Be sure to *never copy and paste* dollar amounts or your electronic AIA pay application *will not* be an accurate automation when entering new billings.
- Essentially, when a pay application is inaccurate, it has great potential to cause contractor payment delays for your company. Thus, interrupting the scheduled cash flow projections for the continued seamless operations of your business.
- As you manipulate through the electronic pay application entries, you will also be able to note automatic numerical updated populations on both pages of the electronic pay application forms G702 and G703.
- In updating the AIA Pay Application Form G702, you should be able to easily understand the totals for your Previous Certificates for Payment listed on line number 7. You should also note that the amount of your last pay application certified payment amount *will always* be listed on the front page of the pay application form G702 in the space titled Current Payment Due or line number 8.
- To verify the new billing month's Previous Certificates for Payment Total, simply add the Current Payment Due amount listed on line number 8 to the Less Previous Certificates for Payment total listed on line number 7.
- There is also a section for change order math computations. This section is titled as Change Order Summary and is located

on the left side of the AIA Application and Certificate for Payment Form G702. Basically, it is self explanatory for data entry changes relating to your project.

- Depending upon the type of project changes you may have, you will either input data for an added dollar amount (the monetary change above your original contract sum) or deductive dollar amount (the monetary change below your original contract sum) for that particular billing month.
- Words of Caution: If you want to be paid for verbal change orders, keep in mind that you must receive such in formal written format with approval signatures by authorized construction project management.
- Verbal agreements with hand shakes simply will not get you paid for project change orders that may result into additional unplanned work for your construction crews. Again, take the time to ensure you are compensated for extra work by <u>never</u> performing additional work until you have first received a formal written and signed change order from the requesting construction project manager. Otherwise, you initiate the very high risk of doing extra work free of charge!
- Progress payments are always determined based upon your best estimated amount owed to your company for work your team has performed and should be paid for that period.
- For clarity purposes, you may also consult with the project manager to better determine how much you should bill for any portion of work for that particular period. Most project managers will mean well in trying to help you figure a fair and just amount to invoice their company for any portion of work that their subcontracting companies perform.
- If ever in doubt with how to use the AIA Application and Certificate for Payment Forms G702 and G703, always refer to the AIA website at www.aia.org for customer support.

- Finally, once AIA Application and Certificate For Payment forms have been accurately completed, you will need to have forms notarized, and accompanied by lien waiver, state sales tax, and any other forms as applicable and required by the project manager, architect or owner prior to submitting for progress payment.
- Always take advantage to attend construction project pre-bid meetings to learn details about the project. These meetings are imperative for asking questions and learning who the contact person should be for submitting monthly application and certificate for payments. These meetings also allow for visual walk-throughs and site visits of the proposed project, as well as, networking opportunities with representatives from other contracting companies.

CHAPTER 7

A Mission Accomplished

Richard and I have been blessed to have been selected as the preferred prime contractor for several private projects. Although Richard's intuition had manifested, I do not think he had any idea as to how much our business would change for the better. God is an awesome promise-keeper! He will allow things to happen in your life that will appear at the outset to be your demise only to bring you into a place of milk and honey. I have learned that if I continue to trust and have faith in the Almighty God, He will always hold me, help me, and allow me to stand on solid foundations.

The only real trickery in learning how to do business in this new commercial construction industry was that it was difficult to know who was really a friend or foe. So many people seemed to have meant well and appeared to have had good business ethics at the ongoing networking meetings and other related business functions. Nonetheless, we could not help but feel that we still needed to watch our backs.

As our business name and reputation began to be acknowledged positively in the contractor community, it became more difficult to determine who was genuinely celebrating with us and who was being kind for ulterior motives. People who never paid us any attention in times past now wanted to know us and acknowledge us publicly. Others wanted to leverage our good business name to appear a certain way in front of large VIP audiences. In this business, one really has to trust the good Lord for guidance and direction. What this means for Richard and me is that God promises that no weapon, absolutely no weapon formed against us shall be able to prosper according to Isaiah 54:17, KJV.

In other words, folks may try to undermine you in business or damage your reputation, but their efforts will have no effect at all. When you build a right relationship with and trust the Lord, he protects you from those who mean harm. The only way one can really trust the Lord is to receive him as their personal Lord and Saviour as written in Romans 10:9-10, KJV, and then the promises of God really become yours personally.

CHAPTER 8

Encouragement for New Beginnings

Never did I imagine on the day that I was laid off from what I thought was secure employment in December 2003 that my world would change into numerous opportunities to conduct entrepreneurial business at astronomical levels. I feel confident in believing that we are well on our way to building one of the best minority contracting companies in the south.

If you have been laid off in this very trying American economy and feel as if you don't know how to make the ends meet economically, I strongly encourage you to trust God. Ask him to be your personal saviour right now, and then ask him for direction. He will lead and guide you and show you exactly what he wants you to do next. Once he shows you trust him for every provision. I'll be the first to say that at times it may look so scary you will find it hard to believe that God told you to do anything at all; you may even find yourself being tempted to question God's clear instructions. However, I'll also be the first to say that if you dare to trust and obey God in making earnest efforts to perform that special task that he has assigned to your hands, he will always provide for the assignment.

Now I know that our construction company was a divine assignment given to my husband by God himself. Presently, we are viewed by the entire city and state as one of the upcoming and successful general contracting companies. Our customer base has grown from residential customers of family and friends to a diverse customer base that regularly spends multiple millions of dollars on new construction procurement.

We now service customers representing local universities, public schools, utility companies, and local and state government agencies. The proof of God's great provisions for us, despite a failing economy, has been the fact that for the past eight years or more, I have not worked anywhere else other than for my husband in his construction business. Instead of losing our home, we have improved and maintained it. Instead of losing our vehicles, we have gained more vehicles. Our house is beautifully sustained, and we are able to make improvements as inspired for the marketing of our construction services. Also, while having been laid off from the workforce, I find it absolutely amazing that my husband and I have actually always thrived in entrepreneurial endeavors even until this day. God is faithful!

In closing, let me just inspire you to never be afraid of job layoffs or failing economies. God is more than able to sustain you if you make him your Lord and Saviour, and then trust him to do so. I encourage you to do whatever it is that he wants you to do, and watch it prosper. Although I felt defeated after losing the only thing I knew as my main source of income, today I truly thank God for having been terminated. Not only was it a major stepping stone and elevation in my career, but it was also the very best thing that could have happened to my husband and me as entrepreneurs! Our business allows us flexibility to become more involved in the community, as well as to be a beacon of light and hope to the less fortunate living within our local community. Our company allows us to reach out to help people who seek to help themselves.

Construction management college students can earn internships with our firm, and the underprivileged can also better themselves through opportunities of employment, education, and apprenticeships, all of which our organization offers its staff members.

I have learned that being a small business owner definitely puts one in a much stronger position than those who rely on traditional employment. The small business owner may have to endure times of economical downturns, but nonetheless, he or she still holds the higher position because of the unlimited cash flow potential business ownership produces.

Once business owners possess unlimited cash flow, they can make a higher impact within various communities by fulfilling selective community responsibilities.

The name of my construction company is Pullen Construction Company, LLC. To learn more about Pullen and to view the construction project gallery, feel free to visit www.pullenconstruction.com.

For this business, Richard and I are eternally grateful to God for all the great things he has done, and is yet doing in the marketplace through our hands. If you have been negatively impacted by failing economies, don't be discouraged. If you have never received the free gift of salvation, start your prayer of communication to the Lord by asking God for his wonderful plan of salvation, and then ask him for his awesome plan for your life. Repent and receive Christ today and watch God lead and guide you into a new life in Christ solely for his purpose. For your convenience and to help you get on the right track, I have included a simple prayer of repentance outlined below. I hope that this publication has been a blessing and source of encouragement to you! God bless you!

Dear Heavenly Father,

I ask you to forgive me of my sins. I believe that you sent your Son, Jesus, to be born of a virgin birth. I also believe that he lived on the earth, was crucified, raised on the third day, and is now seated at the right hand of the Father. Please come and live inside my heart - teach me how to live for you. Please fill me with your Holy Spirit and lead me to a good Christian teaching church, so that I can learn more about you. Thank you for hearing my prayer!

In Jesus Name, Amen

www.ingramcontent.com/pod-product-compliance
Lightning Source LLC
Chambersburg PA
CBHW021452070526
44577CB00002B/377